This book belongs to:

Complete the dot-to-dot and then color the picture.

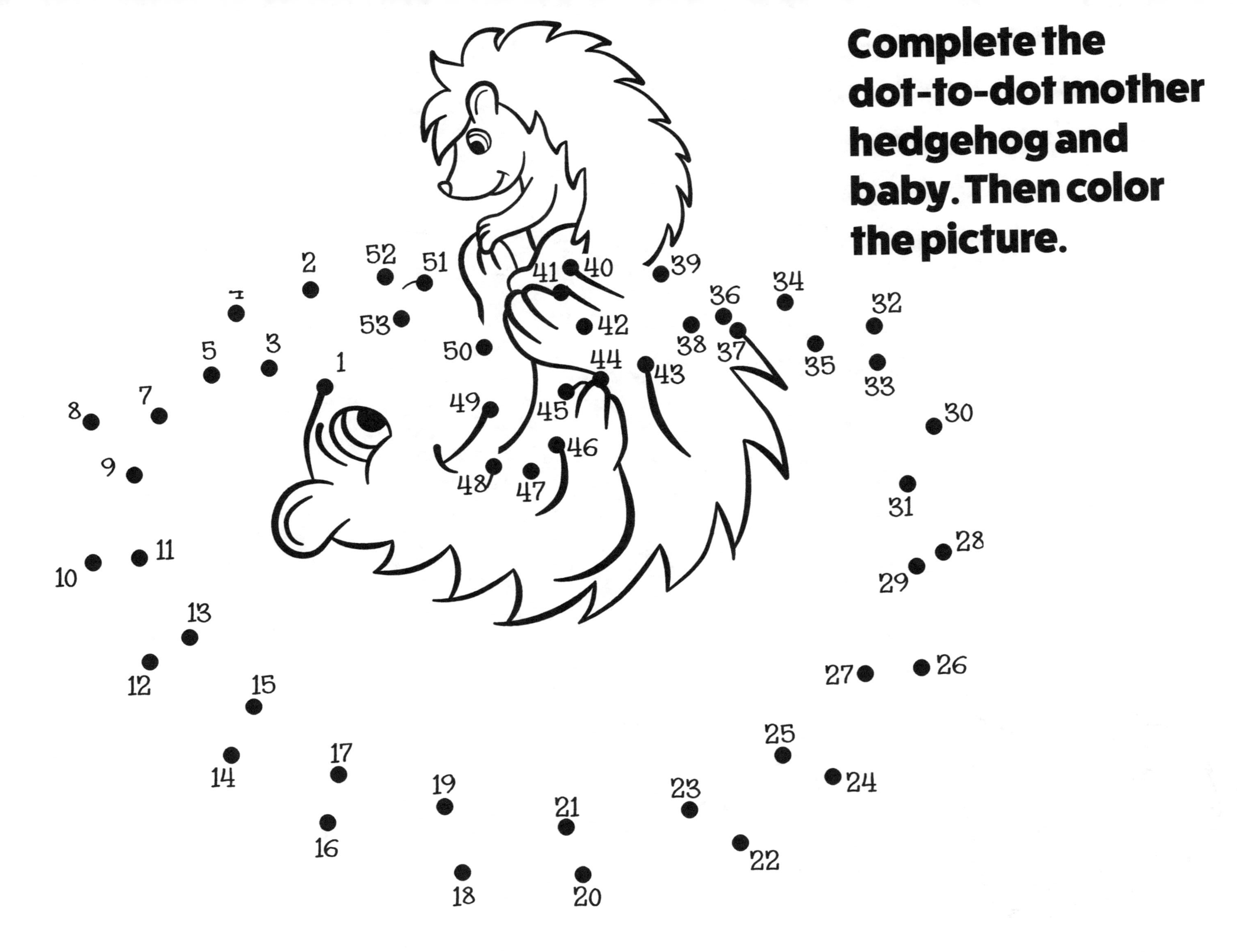

Complete the dot-to-dot mother hedgehog and baby. Then color the picture.

Help the hedgehog reach the basket of mushrooms.

1 - light blue 2 - green 3 - dark green 4 - gray
5 - beige 6 - orange 7 - red 8 - brown

a	e	z	x	p	i	g	h	f	i
m	n	o	p	q	r	s	t	z	v
f	g	h	z	k	y	x	w	l	u
c	b	e	g	x	l	m	o	k	p
a	i	d	m	t	z	y	x	d	t
d	b	g	j	l	i	o	n	o	y
h	f	e	k	j	m	z	y	n	w
e	d	h	y	i	l	o	p	k	x
f	h	o	m	k	x	m	w	e	w
e	i	g	j	l	o	p	q	y	e

Find these words in the WORD SEARCH:

lion **hedgehog**

pig **donkey**

Write ten words from the word hedgehog. Hint: there's 90 possible words (for example, the word goes).

1.

2.

3.

4.

5.

6.

7.

8.

9.

10.

Use the grid to draw and color the sleeping hedgehog!

Complete the maze, so the hedgehog can hide in the vegetables.

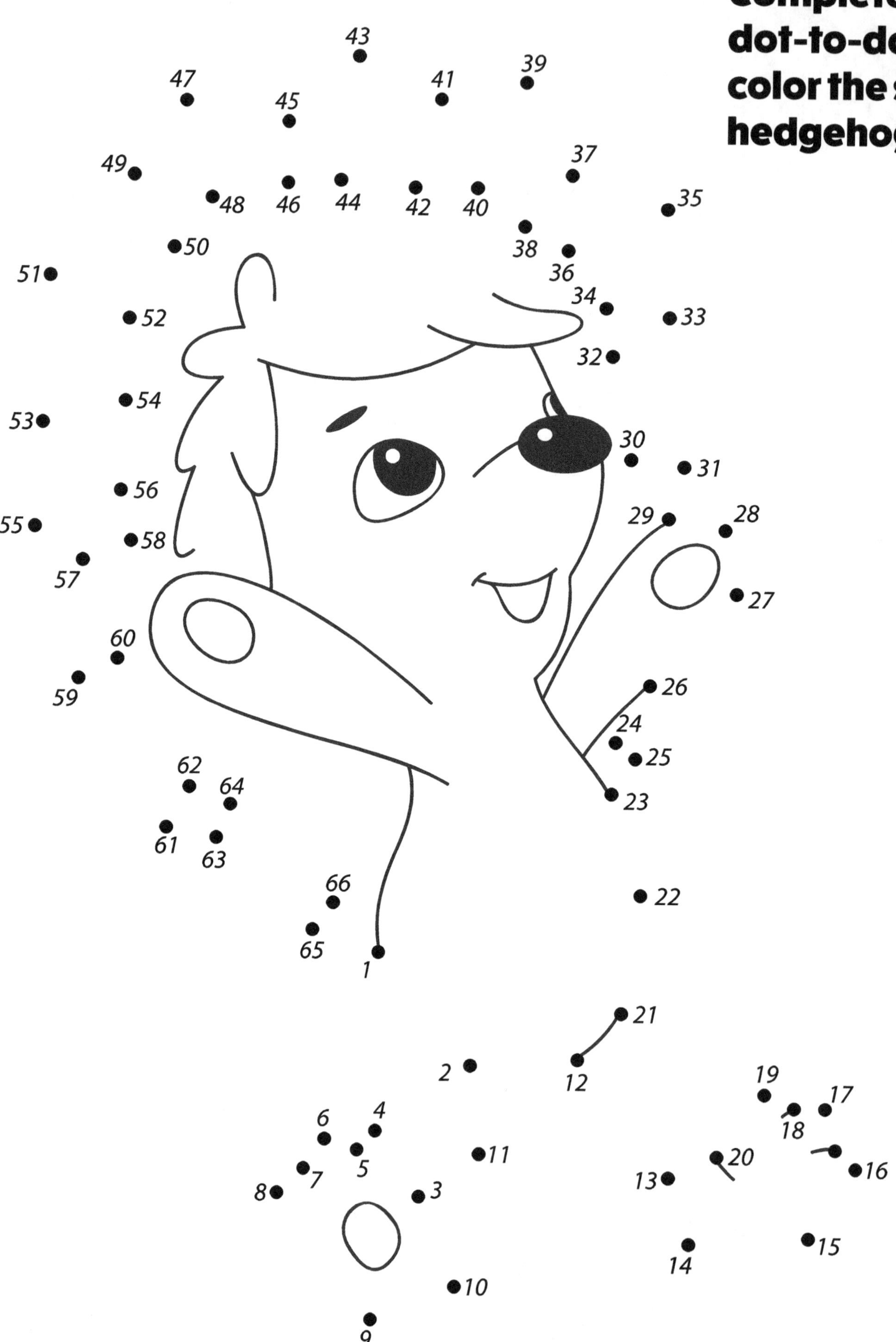

Complete the dot-to-dot and color the silly hedgehog.

Color and name the animals.

Color by Number!

1. dark blue
2. light blue
3. brown
4. tan

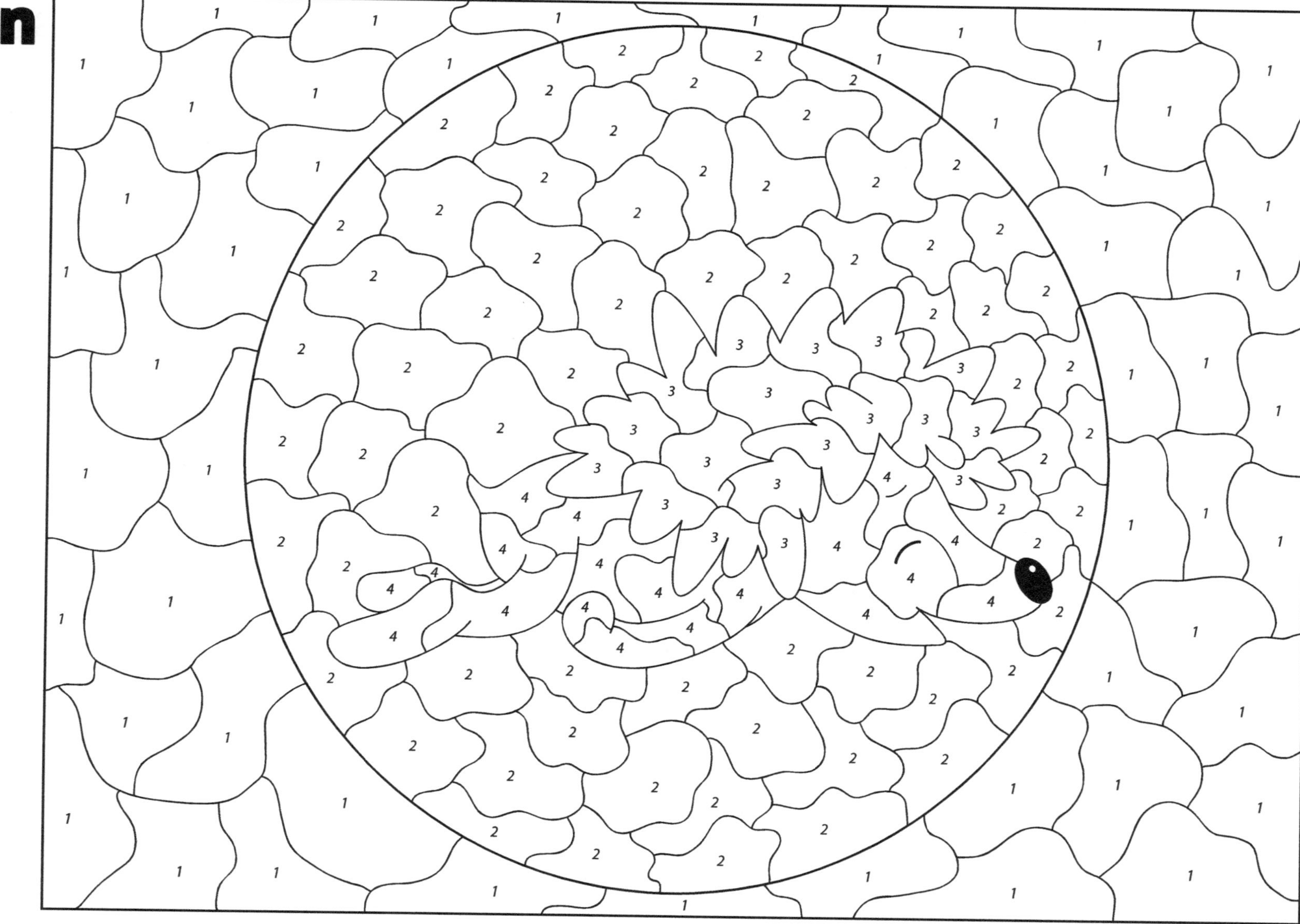

Use the grid to draw and color the silly hedgehog!

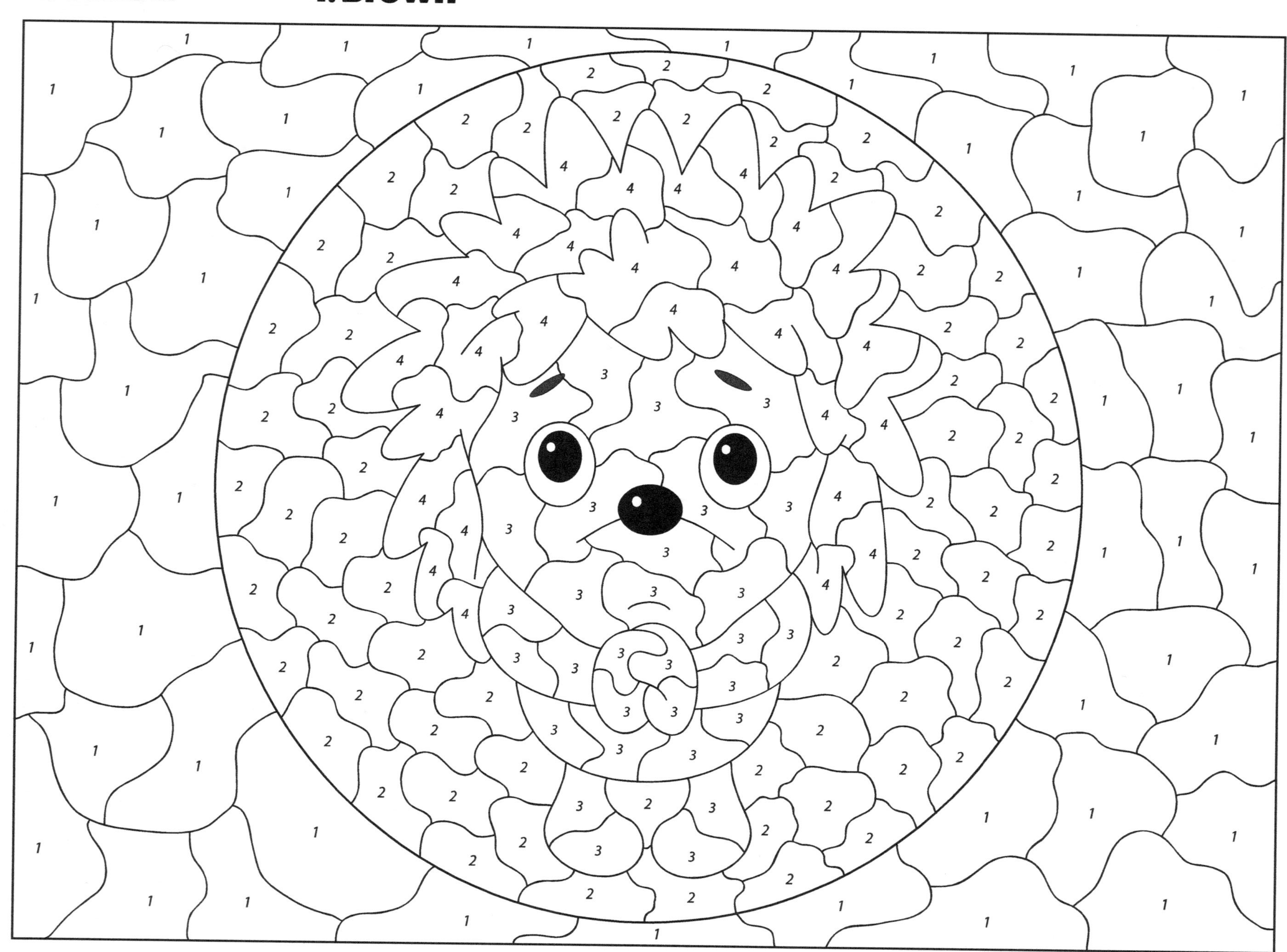

1. Orange
2. Yellow
3. Tan
4. Brown
COLOR BY NUMBER

Use the grid to draw and color the cute hedgehog!

Use the grid to draw and color the delightful hedgehog!

Circle the number of the shadow that matches the hedgehog.

Help the hedgehog reach the mushrooms, so he can hide!

Write another word that starts with a letter from the word mushroom.

1. m-_______________________________

2. u-_______________________________

3. s-_______________________________

4. h-_______________________________

5. r-_______________________________

6. o-_______________________________

7. o-_______________________________

8. m-_______________________________

Connect the dots and color the sad hedgehog!

Color and name the animals. Did you know that hedgehogs are meat-eaters?

Letter Rebus
Write the four animals.

1.

2.

3.

4.

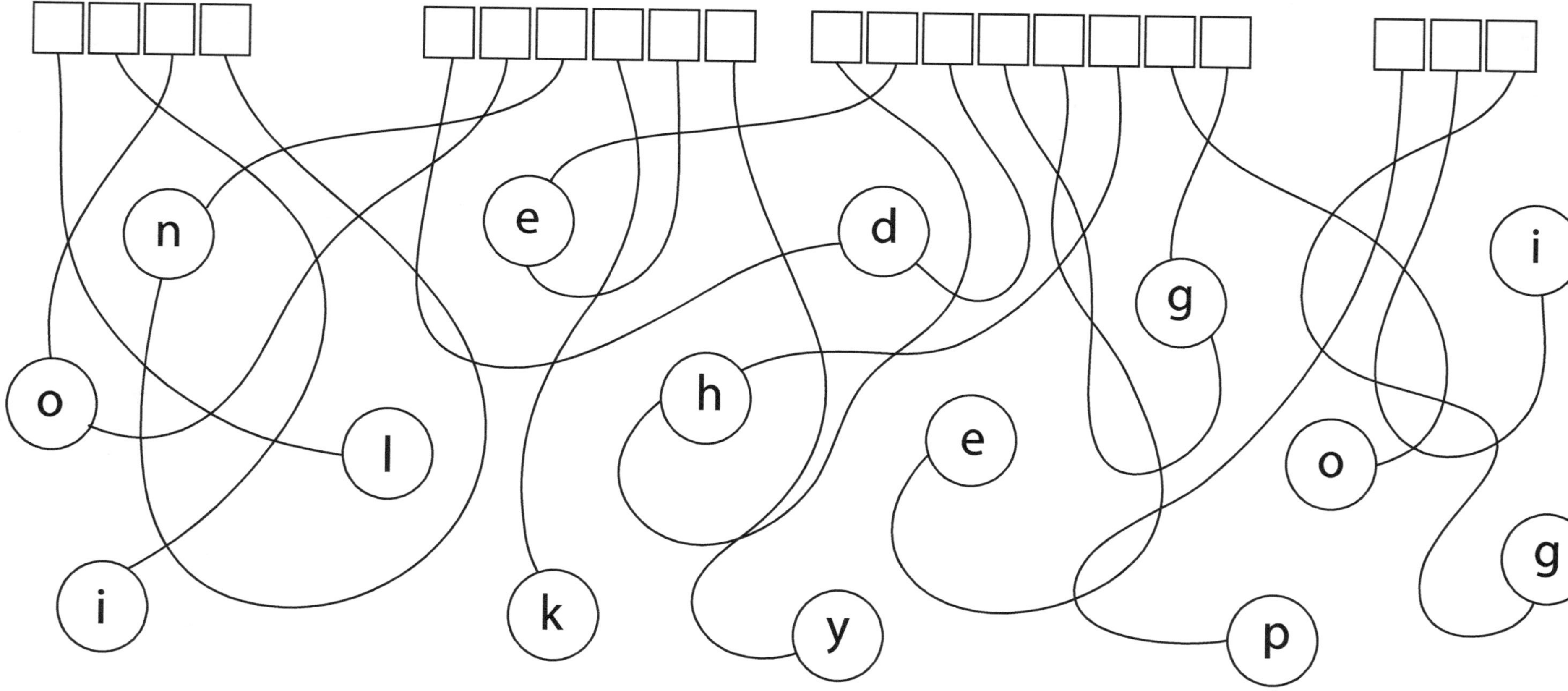

Animal Word Search: WORD BANK

owl   rabbit   fox

deer   squirrel   hedgehog

1 F ☐ ☐
2 O ☐ ☐
3 ☐ ☐ ☐ R
4 ☐ ☐ ☐ ☐ E ☐ ☐ ☐
5 S ☐ ☐ ☐ ☐ ☐ ☐ ☐ ☐
6 ☐ ☐ ☐ ☐ ☐ T

Circle the animals that don't have a match. Then color all of the animals.

The word hedgehog starts with the letter h. Name four other animals that begin with the letter h?

1.

2.

3.

4.

Shadow Matching Game

Forest Animals

- Color the pictures
- Draw the lines matching each picture to its shadow

Help the hedgehog and her babies reach the mushroom!

CUT & GLUE

COLOR
1

CUT OUT
2

GLUE
3

USE EXAMPLE OR YOUR IMAGINATION

CUT & GLUE
COLOR
1
CUT OUT
2
GLUE
3
USE EXAMPLE OR YOUR IMAGINATION

Super Cool Hedgehog Activity Book: Dot-to-Dot, Draw, Coloring, Mazes, Word Search, Color by Number, Matching, & More!

Thank you for your recent purchase. We hope you've enjoyed your Hedgehog Activity Book! If you love hedgehogs, please see our "Super Cool Hedgehogs Facts & Coloring Book" to color & learn more about hedgehogs!
by florabellapublishing.com